ARCTIC OCEAN

COLVILLE RIVER

NOATAK RIVER

KOBUK RIVER

KONUKUK RIVER

YUKON RIVER

FAIRBANKS

NORTON SOUND

YUKON RIVER

TANANA RIVER

MT. McKINLEY

SUSITNA RIVER

KUSKOKWIM RIVER

ANCHORAGE

COPPER RIVER

NUSHAGAK RIVER

KUSKOKWIM BAY

JUNEAU

BRISTOL BAY

GULF OF ALASKA

KODIAK ISLAND

PACIFIC OCEAN

Kenai Fjords National Park

By Andromeda Romano-Lax
Photography by Ron Niebrugge

Alaska Natural History Association
Anchorage, Alaska

Designer: Chris Byrd
Illustrations/Map: Denise Ekstrand
Photography: All photos by Ron Niebrugge except:
      pg. 10,44 Anchorage Museum
      pg. 21 NOAA
      pg. 31 Laura Greffenius
      pg. 38 Joe Meehan
      pg. 38 Art Sowls
      pg. 46,48 NPS
Author: Andromeda Romano-Lax
Series and Book Editor: Nora L. Deans
Agency Coordinator: Sandy Brue
Project Manager: Lisa Oakley
Contributer: Sandy Brue

Alaska Natural History Association is a nonprofit publisher of books and other
materials about Alaska's public lands. For more information or to join: www.alaskanha.org

ALASKA
NATURAL HISTORY ASSOCIATION

750 West Second Avenue, Suite 100
Anchorage, AK 99501
907-274-8440 or 1-866-AK-PARKS
www.alaskanha.org

ISBN: 0-930931-53-X

Library of Congress Cataloging-in-Publication Data
Romano-Lax, Andromeda, 1971-
Kenai Fjords National Park / by Andromeda Romano-Lax.
p. cm.
Includes bibliographical references and index.
ISBN 0-930931-53-X (pbk.)
1.   Natural history-Alaska-Kenai Fjords National Park. 2. Kenai Fjords
National Park (Alaska)--Description and travel. 3. Kenai Fjords National
Park (Alaska)--History. I. Alaska Natural History Association. II. Title.

F912.K4R655 2004
917.98'3--dc22
2004010589

Printed in China on recycled paper.

A Rare Jewel in a Perfect Setting

CONTENTS

KENAI FJORDS NATIONAL PARK

The Fog Lifts

Imagine the terror of ice-choked waters in a day of wooden ships. Imagine how the idea of a coast reshaping itself year after year – confounding one's ideas of permanency, predictability, and scale – would have jostled the nerves of an early navigator along the shores of what would become Kenai Fjords National Park.

The echoing boom of calving ice, audible for miles, would have added white-knuckle tension to an already wearying sail along a poorly mapped coastline. The whir of a clown-faced puffin, flapping furiously overhead, might have provided some comic relief, but only temporarily, until the fog descended, enshrouding a ship in dread.

Most European explorers preferred to keep a safe distance from the Kenai Peninsula's jagged southern coast, which was less welcoming than broadly indented Cook Inlet to the northwest and Prince William Sound to the east. In 1794, explorer George Vancouver described the outer coast west of Seward as

having a "much more wintry aspect than the countries bordering on those more northern inland waters we had so recently quitted."

Fjords that stretch miles inland today were still buried in ice. McCarty Fjord calved within view of the open Gulf of Alaska. Aialik Bay was – and is – guarded by gnarled capes, and often obscured by cloud and storm.

In an 1852 atlas, Mikhail Teben'kov, chief manager of the Russian American Company, summed up the known cartography of the region, labeling the coast's bays and straits as "inconvenient." Even Voskresenskaia (now Resurrection) Bay, he wrote, was marked by a "severity of climate, wildness of nature and inaccessible bottom."

The Russian fur hunters who dominated this coast for most of a century realized that the fjords were neither impenetrable nor unpeopled. Yet even to them it was a no-man's-land – a transitional stretch of coast, dividing more temperate regions to the west and east. Though Russian traders established a fort at Alexandrovsk (today called Nanwalek) and a shipyard in Resurrection Bay, they gave the region between those locations no special name and recorded few of its wonders, thereby shrouding the outer coast in a different sort of fog.

Since the period of European exploration and Russian colonialization that ended in 1867, glaciers have retreated. Fjords have lengthened and deepened. A thin band of spruce, hemlock, and avalanche-resistant alder have reclaimed land liberated from ice. The land itself has changed. So have our ideas.

Today, the fog is lifting. We know now that the outer coast – forbidding to an English or Spanish boat captain; "inconvenient" to a Russian manager; seemingly empty even in the minds of some early American observers – was in fact home to a versatile people called the Unegkurmiut. Their adaptations have much to teach us. Their ability to live lightly and travel far challenges us

to think of the fjords not as an isolated pocket of forbidding wilderness, but as one link in a long cultural chain extending from the Aleutian Islands to Southeast Alaska, along which peoples mixed and migrated, traded and warred.

Using the Kenai Fjords National Park as both archive and living laboratory, we're learning more than early explorers could have dreamed about the science of glaciers, the lives of harbor seals and orcas, the ways that continents sink and forests rebound. We're discovering, in the face of humbling seascapes and ancient ice, a place not for terror, but for wonder.

The same elements that once discouraged explorers now attract visitors. Along a coast of crashing ice and stirred waters, this most ancient of landscapes reveals itself in new and awe-inspiring ways.

People of the Fjords

"Ay-yah!" That exhalation of surprise crosses cultures and echoes through time. It may be the sound early Native settlers made upon rounding a rocky, wave-beaten cape and discovering... unexpectedly mirror-calm water. A maze of ice floes. Hundreds of seals. And an immense, glowing wall of blue ice. The glacier rumbles like distant thunder. Again: "Ay-yah!"

"Aialik," an extension of those first two startled syllables, probably means "scary place," says archaeologist Aron Crowell. What made this easternmost fjord so frightening? Was it the process of navigating around its exposed eastern cape? Some aspect of the inner bay's scenery? Or something else entirely, such as the presence of a resident shaman? We don't know. But the name, said with trepidation or simple delight, still feels right on our tongues. When a glacier calves or a whale's back suddenly splits the water's glittering surface: "Ay-yah!"

Hidden History

Perhaps more surprising than Kenai Fjords scenery is the fact that people lived here at all. The signs – house depressions cloaked in cow parsnip, scarred trees – are invisible to most visitors. To the east and west, Prince William Sound, Kachemak Bay, and the Kodiak Archipelago are all better studied, with archaeological efforts dating back to the 1930s. By comparison, the human history of the Kenai's outer coast has remained obscure. Yet it is rich, spanning at least a thousand years, with living connections to the memories and traditions of Native residents in Nanwalek and Port Graham, just west of the national park's boundaries.

A three-year archaeology project, begun in 2002, has launched the first substantial excavations of outer coast sites once inhabited by the Unegkurmiut, a Chugach Alutiiq subgroup. This exciting effort combines fieldwork – a window into the distant past – with oral history – a bridge to living memory.

More than thirty indigenous archaeology sites, dating back to AD 250, have been identified in Kenai Fjords National Park and on adjacent Nuka Island. At excavations like this one, scientists, students, and elders gather to record and interpret the findings.

Alutiiq elders have returned recently to places where their grandparents or great-grandparents may have lived, hunted, and paddled. The elders offer insights, distilled from tradition, that help archaeologists interpret new findings. An archaeologist wonders: Why are bone fragments so abundant in a firepit? A Native villager answers: because of the custom, called "pinahsuhtut" or "hunting for good weather," of tossing bones into the cooking fire to chase away storms. Why is a long-abandoned house so well stocked with tools? Perhaps, elders suggest, because the Alutiiq follow a hospitable tradition of leaving houses well stocked with food, firewood, and tools that might be needed by travelers seeking emergency shelter.

The Cove Site, one of the oldest known sites in the Park, holds clues to the outer coast's dynamic nature. Near the bottom of the excavation site, charcoal remains indicate human occupation as early as AD 1020. People may have used the fjords even earlier, but the signs have been hidden – not only by the passage of time, but by the advance of glaciers and seismic warping of shorelines.

In the last 5,000 years, a time of flourishing culture along the Gulf of Alaska, the Kenai coast dropped six to eight times, drowning many clues to early fjord habitation. One of these catastrophic plunges, however, did leave its mark on the Cove Site. A lens of wave-deposited gravel recalls a massive earthquake that rocked the coast in about AD 1170. This earthquake was stronger than Alaska's 1964 earthquake, causing subsidence throughout the region. At Aialik Bay, the shore sank nearly six feet. Tsunami waves probably flooded the fjords.

Near the top of the Cove Site pit, a layer shows that people had returned a century later, when the land had risen slightly. Near the top of the excavation, a layer of ash records a volcanic explosion of 500 years ago.

Earthquakes, tsunamis, volcanic eruptions: these were only some of the natural forces that Cove Site dwellers faced. Elsewhere in the fjords, life was no less dramatic. Settlement of Harris Bay ended abruptly 200 years ago when the face of Northwestern Glacier approached to less than a thousand yards of the site. The Little Ice Age would not relinquish its grip on the outer coast until 1900, when glaciers in many of the fjords reached today's limit.

In addition to geological changes, outer coast residents contended with long-term biological fluctuations. Seals and sea lions, typical Alutiiq food sources, might be abundant in one generation, and less so in the next. These changes were more complex than simply "fat" or "lean" years. Scientists are beginning to understand that Gulf of Alaska marine populations appear to shift in natural cycles of 20 to 50 years. These cycles are linked to periods of oceanic warming and cooling, with cold cycles favoring animals like herring, capelin, and shrimp, and warmer cycles favoring fish that are higher on the food chain, including salmon and pollock.

Old village and campsite bone middens are biological archives, containing fish and mammal bones that archaeologists can use to study these natural cycles. In the Kenai Fjords National Park, archaeologists will be using these bones and the isotopes they contain to show how water temperatures have changed, how animals have increased or declined, and how those animals changed their feeding patterns. The results will not only explain more about Alutiiq life, but will add a piece to the larger North Pacific climate puzzle.

From Kayaks to Baidarkas

Cataclysms and climate changes aside, what was life like for an outer coast dweller? While inhabited, the region was probably less densely populated than neighboring areas. Kodiak Island, for example, has larger salmon runs. The fjords have steep shorelines, with few places to land. And there were further limitations. A site at the head of a bay would mean no escape if a warring party invaded. Many beaches that look appealing now were covered by glaciers as recently as a century ago. Despite these restrictions, at least nine former village sites have been located in the fjords.

Signs of cataclysm and change abound along the coast. Where earthquakes have rattled the land and caused shorelines to subside, salt water floods the coastal forest, creating stands of dead "ghost trees."

"People Out That Way"

Prince William Sound neighbors called the people of the Kenai's outer coast "Unegkurmiut," meaning "People Out That Way." But no record exists to tell us what outer coast people called themselves, and descendants in Nanwalek and Port Graham don't identify themselves with the Unegkurmiut label. "Chugach," a broader term, refers to the Pacific Eskimo people of Cook Inlet, Kenai Peninsula coast, and Prince William Sound. The umbrella terms "Alutiiq" and "Sugpiaq" extend farther yet, including Pacific Eskimos from the Alaska Peninsula all the way to Prince William Sound, and a cultural heritage of 7,000 years.

Because these sites were not necessarily closest to hunting grounds or plant-gathering areas, skin-covered boats were essential for Unegkurmiut people, just as they were for other Alutiiq peoples. The original Chugach Alutiiq kayak had room for one or two paddlers, with a third seat added in post-contact times for Russian overseers, who called the small boats "baidarkas." Larger boats, capable of transporting up to 20 or 30 people, were called "angyaqs." Traveling by kayak and wearing transparent, waterproof overgarments sewn from animal intestines, a hunter could pursue otters, seals, sea lions, and whales. On land, he could hunt bears, goats, marmots, and other small mammals. By eating a diverse diet and traveling lightly, outer coast people were able to cope with an ever-changing environment.

Russian fur companies based in Nanwalek depended upon outer coast residents to catch fur-bearing mammals from first contact through the decline of the fur trade. Introduced diseases devastated outer coast residents, as they plagued Native peoples throughout Alaska.

After the Russian period ended, Native residents of Yalik, on the west side of today's Park, continued to hunt furs for the Alaska Commercial Company. Where the earliest Russian profiteers relied on physical force to control the Native Aleut population, later Russian and American entrepreneurs subdued the Alutiiq population in different ways. Most sea otter hunters became indebted quickly to the company store, where they were issued kayaks, hunting equipment, food and luxury goods on credit. Eventually, the collapse of fur prices, rise of commercial fishing and creation of a cash economy lured families away from the fjords to more centralized trading posts and company towns. Relocation was encouraged by officials of the Russian Orthodox Church, a faith that many Nanwalek and Port Graham residents embrace today. An 1880 census reported 32 people at Yalik, one of the last permanent villages within the Park. By 1890, no record of the population remained. Still, Alutiiq people based in villages farther west continued to fish and hunt the fjords seasonally as late as the 1940s.

The village of Nanwalek sold its property rights to areas in the National Park in the 1990s as part of a habitat protection program. At this time, Port Graham still retains its property rights. Both villages retain some subsistence use and cultural rights within the Park. Descendants of the fjords' original dwellers still nurture a sense of attachment to their ancestral lands.

"When the tide is out the table is set"

Like their outer coast ancestors, Nanwalek and Port Graham residents harvest an astonishing variety of foods from the sea, including not only salmon and halibut, but also seal and sea lion, which are shared by virtually every household in both villages, according to state surveys. Residents gather eggs, wild plants, seaweeds, and marine invertebrates. Bottom-dwelling species that can be harvested with spears or by hand are called uyangtaaq, and include clams, cockles, mussels, snails, chitons (called "bidarkies") and octopus. Harvesting the tidal shallows is an especially beloved activity because it can be shared by the youngest and eldest villagers.

"One learns that the world, though made, is yet being made.
That this is still the morning of creation."

—John Muir

Braving the Elements

Several years ago, Park Resource Management Specialist Mike Tetreau and three companions were crossing the Harding Icefield when a storm struck. Sky overhead and ground underfoot yielded to white. Driving snow blotted out everything, even the black nunataks – or "lonely peaks" – that protrude hundreds of feet above the vast ice. The wind blew strong enough to roll the 50-pound sleds the travelers were towing behind them.

Anyone who ventures into backcountry Alaska expects some precipitation. The question is how much. And for how long. Waiting out the snowstorm in a tent might seem like a comfortable option. Except that Tetreau's tent was completely buried every two-and-a-half hours. Digging out might seem merely wearying. Except the storm's passing was followed by another storm, and another, rolling in from the Gulf of Alaska, where a mighty climatic engine spins throughout the seasons, pushing moisture-laden ocean air toward the mountainous coast. The air rises thousands of feet, cools, and drops its snowy cargo – sometimes for days on end.

With storm conditions continuing, there was no way for Tetreau and friends to wait, or to retreat. The adventurers simply had to "suck it up and push on," skiing through windblown snow to the icefield's easiest escape route, at aptly named Exit Glacier, the endpoint for most icefield crossings.

During the three days the party slogged, more than ten feet of snow fell. In a year, the Harding Icefield is blanketed by an estimated 400 to 800 inches. Compare that to Alaska's north slope – technically a desert – where less than 10 inches of precipitation is the norm.

This bounty of snowfall has a greater hand in shaping Kenai Fjords National Park than any other natural force. The same snowstorm that flattens a tent in hours can bury wayward airplanes in a day or two. The same snow compressed into ice can do even more: bulldoze a forest, plow a U-shaped valley, deepen a fjord. Few climbers venture across the icefield; in some years, none at all. But hundreds of thousands of Park visitors see the icefield's progeny: the fissured face of Exit Glacier, or the sheer walls of glacier-carved bays.

Tidewater and landlocked glaciers behave differently. The retreat of tidewater glaciers, which can be dramatic, is not solely dependent on climate. Many other factors control how a glacier recedes, including the topography of a glacier's fjord. Once a tidewater glacier has become free of its moraine – the seafloor sediment pile that anchors it to the bottom of the fjord – its retreat accelerates. The retreat may be slow, or it may reverse, once the glacier has backed out of the water. Both coming and going, tidewater glaciers act like spring-loaded rubber bands, shooting forward and back faster than year-to-year weather conditions might suggest.

Alaska's glaciers are melting, like Holgate Glacier in Aialik Bay. A ten-year study reported in the Anchorage Daily News *showed that runoff from Alaska's glaciers contributed twice as much fresh water to the world's oceans as the giant Greenland ice sheet. But melting and other forms of ablation are only one side of the glacier equation. Accumulation, from increased precipitation, for example, may or may not balance the other side. Climate change will continue to affect the state's glaciers – perhaps in unexpected and complicated ways.*

Crowned by Ice

Twenty thousand years ago, during the Pleistocene Epoch, glaciers covered half of Alaska. Now, they cover only five percent. Modest as it may seem, that percentage translates into lots of ice: the state may have about 100,000 glaciers – 99 percent of them unnamed – and has four massive icefields. One of these, the Harding Icefield, dominates Kenai Fjords National Park like an icy crown. Possibly thousands of feet thick and interrupted by unglaciated mountain peaks, it covers 700 square miles and feeds 38 glaciers, all of them in a constant state of flux.

A glacier is created in an area when more snow falls than melts. The accumulated snow pack thickens, and the snowflakes themselves change, losing their six-sided, crystalline form. After surviving one summer melt season, the flakes have become a material called firn. The firn is further compressed over years or even decades, until it is nine times denser than the original snow. Little air is trapped inside the glacier ice, but what does remain is subject to intense pressure. As calved icebergs melt, the release of air fills the fjords with unworldly sizzling and popping sounds.

As a glacier grows, its own weight becomes a formidable force, pushing the ice downslope. This surprisingly fluid movement is why glaciers are called "rivers of ice." Like a river, glaciers don't move at a uniform pace, or in a uniform fashion. The center of a glacier moves more quickly than its edges, for example. Deep within the glacier, a zone of "plastic flow" allows the ice to move more easily; but at the brittle top layer, enormous cracks form. These crevasses can be over 100 feet deep.

As glaciers flow, they reshape the underlying bedrock in two ways. First, the glacier can pluck boulders outright, depositing them as erratics in unexpected places. Second, the glacier drags along a layer of rock debris. In sandpaper-like fashion, this abrasive layer grinds bedrock into rock flour – a fine sediment that colors outwash streams brown, milky white, or an opaque and unearthly blue-green. Like sandpaper rubbed repeatedly over an unfinished surface, a glacier erodes a valley both coming and going. Repeated advances and recessions of glaciers wear away mountains and deepen fjords. This geological two-step is powered by a global climate that has wobbled between cold and warm for millions of years.

Just because all glaciers flow doesn't mean they advance, necessarily. A glacier's mass balance is determined by the sum of accumulation – including the addition of new snow and ice – and ablation – the loss of ice that occurs through melting, calving, and other processes.

The most recent cold snap, the Little Ice Age, lasted from about 1250 to 1900 in Alaska. During this time, tidewater glaciers in the fjords reached their most recent maximum positions: Aialik Glacier in about 1600; Northwestern Glacier, Bear Glacier and others at the turn of the last century. Now they, like all glaciers in the Park, are retreating.

In the late 1800s, McCarty Glacier calved within view of the Gulf of Alaska. The glacier retreated steadily over the decades, reaching a relative gallop of just under a mile a year between 1942 and 1950. As the ice withdrew, McCarty Fjord filled with seawater. Where European explorers would have seen a towering plug of ice, and where early American geologists glimpsed a parting of an icy curtain, there is now a 21-mile-long fjord, filled with sparkling blue water.

Exit Glacier Science

Less than two decades ago, tape measures and simple metal stakes were the surveying tools; today, global positioning systems and laser technology deliver higher-tech appraisals of terminus position and overall "mass balance." The findings in a nutshell? Exit Glacier flows downslope at about one-and-a-half feet a day. But it melts even faster. Since 1950, the glacier face has retreated 1,800 feet – but not uniformly. Between the 1970s to 1993, the glacier actually reversed course and advanced the length of a football field. Reversing yet again, the glacier retreated at an impressive pace. In 2002 alone, the terminus withdrew more than 300 feet – or close to one foot a day.

The landlocked glacier, which can be reached on foot, is seen by over 100,000 visitors annually. Beyond the posted signs, which caution visitors not to approach the terminus, danger lurks. Car-sized chunks of ice have tumbled from the terminus, threatening visitors who don't take the hazards seriously.

Other Forces at Work

All this talk of snowstorms and mountaineers, water and ice, serves to remind us that Kenai Fjords National Park is a dynamic place, reshaped year after year. But sometimes the changes are even more sudden and catastrophic. Just as glaciers flow, the entire surface of the earth – a jigsaw of massive continental and oceanic plates – is on the move.

Southern Alaska is one of the most tectonically active regions on earth, located at the place where two of these massive plates collide. The Pacific Plate moves northward at a rate of about two inches a year. Along the coast, it slips under the lighter North American Plate, compressing and pulling the edge of the lighter plate down with it. Geologists call this process subduction, and it drags the Kenai Mountains into the sea. Lower snow-lines and rising sea level – facts of life during the warmer phases of earth's ever-wobbling climate cycles – further dramatize the effect.

In nearby western Prince William Sound, a hiker could clamber a thousand feet to behold alpine landscapes. In the Kenai Fjords, these same rugged landscapes are visible just yards above sea level – and in places, below it. Cirques – bowl-shaped depressions that once cradled alpine glaciers – are common below sea level along the outer coast.

The unusually wide subduction zone along Alaska's southern coast makes it especially prone to earthquakes, like the one that rocked Seward on March 27, 1964. The Good Friday earthquake measured 8.6 on the Richter scale (upgraded to 9.2 on the moment magnitude scale) and dropped the shoreline six feet. But tremors shook this area long before any scale was invented. Great earthquakes probably caused southern Alaskan shorelines to plunge six to eight times in the last 4,700 years. Life for the region's earliest settlers was further complicated by volcanic eruptions from the dozens of smokers lining the Alaska Peninsula, to the west.

While geological processes tend to be notoriously slow and difficult to observe, the Kenai Fjords offer tangible proof on a human scale: landscape changes. Ice and rocks plow. Plates shift. The evidence is quiet as a ghost forest, where dead, saltwater-indundated trees indicate a seismic dip in the shoreline, or as noisy as a calving glacier. In the wake of these dynamic processes, the world is reborn.

This photo was taken at Seward at the north end of Resurrection Bay, after tsunamis. It shows an overturned ship, demolished Texaco chemical truck, and the torn-up dock strewn with logs and scrap metal. The waves left a wreckage of houses and boats in the lagoon area; some still looked relatively undamaged and some were completely destroyed. The total damage to port and harbor facilities at Seward was estimated at more than $14 million. Most of this damage was the result of the tsunamis. Twelve persons lost their lives due to the sea waves at Seward.

Succession

Mountain peaks may symbolize man's drive to triumph over rock and ice. But the proof of life's true regenerative spirit is found in a humbler place: deglaciated valleys. Where glaciers have receded, baring the rawest terrain known on earth, life nonetheless returns. The orderly way in which this happens is called "succession." First studied in 1887, scientists consider succession one of the most important ideas in the field of ecology. Retreating glaciers, like Exit Glacier, provide an incomparable natural laboratory for studying the predictable stages and organic relationships that allow life to take hold.

Close to the glacier, just beyond jumbled bare rock and twisting creek channels, one sees the first pioneer, lichen. Lacking true stems or roots, this crusty non-plant – actually two organisms, algae and fungi, living as one – needs no soil. It excels, instead, at creating it, by breaking up the rock along which it spreads. Into this thin new soil, seeds are deposited by the winds. Dwarf fireweed, willow, fast-growing alder and young cottonwoods colonize formerly rocky terrain, transforming it into a green patchwork, flagged with fireweed's pink flowers. These plants' roots, in turn, further stabilize the soil and enrich it with nitrogen fixed from the air. Over time, cottonwood trees mature, finally shading and overtaking the smaller willow and alder. For decades more the cottonwoods reign, until they, in turn, are overtaken by other trees: shade-loving Sitka spruce and hemlock, which represent the mature or "climax" stage of this glacial foreland forest. The entire process, from first lichens to towering spruce, takes about 200 years.

Just as plants reclaim and transform new ice-free habitats, so do animals. The Delusion Creek drainage in McCarty Fjord was formed between 1942 and 1980, as McCarty Glacier receded. Already, three species of salmon and Dolly Varden (a salmonid cousin) and the insects on which they feed have recolonized the stream system. Each year, as salmon return to spawn and die, they further enrich their watery homelands.

Lichens break rock into soil, preparing the way for true plants to follow.

*"One learns a landscape finally not by knowing the name or identity
of everything in it, but by perceiving the relationships in it...."*

—Barry Lopez

Life On The Edge

Consider the shape of the Kenai Fjords coast. It is a place of spiky edges and scored rock. Narrow, cove-notched peninsulas end in splayed rock fingers reaching toward the sea.

Or here's another way to see it. A traditional story suggests an octopus-like sea monster shaped this coast with its long-legged thrashing. Studying a map, you can imagine the coast's skinny fjords as impressions left by writhing tentacles. You can picture each of the coast's 40 to 60 embayments as the welts left by great suckers.

It's a complicated geometry. The underwater view, if we could see it, would be even more so. Layers of fresh glacial runoff mix with layers of salty seawater. Cold, nearshore upwellings of nutrient-rich water mix with more temperate water that has traveled in a counter-clockwise eddy split from a distant current, originating near Japan. How do we connect such a complicated physical picture with the lives of the animals that thrive here? What does an oceanographically complex coastline have to do with plankton and puffins, Steller sea lions and tidepool-scavenging black bears?

It's all about food.

Food is what lures bears down narrow valleys, to the water's twisting edge. Food is what lures puffins – birds that spend entire winters offshore – to craggy islets, where they nest and raise their hungry young.

Fish schools form in bays and at undersea ridges. Salmon migrate upriver – but not far, since along the steep outer coast, rivers are short. Currents push prey toward island passages and around headlands. Calving glacial ice stirs the fjord seafloor, sending up plankton and other sealife for birds to eat. Shrimp rise toward the light through sediment-filled water – where they are snatched by young seals.

At the fertile edge where rock and ice tumble into the sea, all manner of animals convene for summer's brief, raucous feast. Few species seem to mind each others' company, which pleases people. With luck we can spot birds, whales and maybe even some of the Park's land dwellers, all within one panoramic frame.

There is life away from the coast, too, of course. On the northeast side of the Park, wolves prowl river valleys. Mountain goats frequent shoreline cliffs, but they also nimbly travel farther inland where few animals – or people – can follow. In winter, wolverines, one of Alaska's most reclusive species, visit the young forest regenerating in the shadow of Exit Glacier's centuries-long retreat. Even on the mile-high Harding Icefield, iceworms prove that life finds a way. But the coast demonstrates best what ecologists call the "edge effect:" where ecosystems overlap, as they do along the coast, diversity peaks.

Even rockbound animals manage to grab their share of the moveable feast. Barnacles are protected by six outer and four inner plates, which close when exposed to air, and open when the tide returns. While tidally submerged, feathery appendages (technically, modified "legs") sweep the nutrient-rich current, collecting drifting plankton and detritus. The barnacles, in turn, are eaten by sea stars.

Bears

Pilots passing over Park glaciers occasionally spot bear tracks – proof that even mountains and miles of ice won't keep a bear from finding its way to a good meal. For the mostly vegetarian black bears, grasses and berries are the food of choice, but they'll eat shellfish, small mammals, and even moose calves. Brown bears thrive on salmon, supplemented with anything from roots to rodents.

Both brown and black bears make use of the Park's many diverse habitats. Since the outer coast's salmon runs are relatively weak, black bears reign there, while brown bears thrive further northeast, in the thickly wooded and salmon-rich Resurrection River valley. But populations may be shifting, and there's much scientists want to know about the movements and habits of each species.

Over the last several years, scientists have radio-collared over 40 black bears along the coast. Transmissions from the collars allow scientists to track where black bears travel and feed, and how the bears react to the presence of human visitors. In another study, researchers are setting traps to snag bear hair. DNA extracted from the hair follicles will help land managers know more about local bear populations.

Group Living

In sheer numbers, the seabirds rule this knife-edged coast where land and roiling waters meet. This avian sovereignty has a democratic side: They've adapted their nesting behaviors to make it possible for many species to coexist peacefully in mixed colonies of limited space. Seabirds spend most of their lives on the open ocean. Each spring, millions of them migrate to shores all along Alaska. Oily fish, like capelin, sand lance, and young herring, draw them to the Kenai Fjords. Cliffs and offshore islands provide the birds with easy access to fish-rich waters below, as well as protected sites to nest and raise their young. In colonies between Aialik Bay and Nuka Island,

In a Park half-covered by ice, space is limited. That's especially true for black oystercatchers, birds that nest on the same narrow beaches prized by kayakers and campers. In recent years, reproductive success has been low, with only a fraction of eggs hatching, and even fewer birds surviving to fledging age. While studies continue, Park managers are trying to help campers avoid sensitive nesting areas.

scientists have tallied about 55,000 adult breeding birds representing 17 species – and that doesn't count birds that nest inland or avoid large groups.

The most recognizable outer coast birds all come from one family: the alcids. Cousins of the penguin, local alcids walk upright due to the rear positioning of their legs. Most have black and white plumages that are variations on the penguins' tuxedo-themed appearance. Unlike penguins, local alcids can fly – but not as well as they can swim.

Taking off is a challenge for the puffin. From land, it makes use of gravity's assistance, plunging from a clifftop to acquire sufficient flying momentum. From sea, it requires a clumsy running start, feet paddling the water until it manages to become airborne. Even underway, the puffin's frantic stubby wingbeats and splayed orange feet lend a comical air. But underwater, it is a graceful swimmer and keen predator. The puffin can catch and carry a dozen or more small fish at a time in its serrated beak.

Two kinds of puffins are seen along the outer coast. Both have large orange or yellow-orange bills that change not only color but shape, becoming brighter and more massive during the breeding season. The tufted puffin, named for the yellow feathers sweeping back from its eyes, is larger than the horned puffin, whose clownlike face is instantly recognizable. From a distance, the easiest way to tell them apart is to look for the horned puffin's white chest and underside. Tufted puffins, by contrast, have solid black bodies. Puffins prefer to nest in tight, cozy spaces: burrows for the tufted puffins, naturally occurring rock crevices for the horned puffins.

Tufted puffins are one of the area's most frequently spotted seabirds. Their brightly colored outer bills and yellow tufts, adapted to attract mates, are shed each fall.

Sampling of Species

Masked shrew (*Sorex cinerus*)

Arctic shrew (*Sorex arcticus*)

Dusky shrew (*Sorex obscurus*)

Northern water shrew (*Sorex palustris*)

Pygmy shrew (*Microsorex hoyi*)

Little brown bat (*Myotus lucifugus*)

Black bear (*Ursus americanus*)

Brown bear (*Ursus arctos*)

Marten (*Martes americana*)

Short-tailed weasel (*Mustela erminea*)

Mink (*Mustela vison*)

River otter (*Lutra canadensis*)

Wolverine (*Gulo luscus*)

Coyote (*Canis latrans*)

Wolf (*Canis lupus*)

Lynx (*Lynx canadensis*)

Hoary marmot (*Marmota caligata*)

Red squirrel (*Tamiasciurus hudsonicus*)

Northern flying squirrel (*Glaucomys sabrinus*)

Beaver (*Castor canadensis*)

Northern bog lemming (*Synaptomys borealis*)

Red-backed vole (*Cleithrionomys rutilis*)

Meadow vole (*Microtus pennsylvanicus*)

Tundra vole (*Microtus oeconomus*)

Meadow jumping mouse (*Zapus hudsonius*)

Porcupine (*Erethizon dorsatum*)

Snowshoe hare (*Lepus americanus*)

Moose (*Alces alces*)

Mountain goat (*Oreamnos americanus*)

Mountain goats travel coastal cliffs and high, wind-swept ridges, where they feed on grasses and shrubs. In stormy winter weather, they seek shelter in spruce stands at timberline. Clockwise from top: wolf, black bears, and hoary marmot.

Harbor Seals in Peril

It's not easy growing up along a fjord's ever-changing edge. For a harbor seal, born at the face of tidewater glaciers, even nursery life is disconcerting. The bassinet – an iceberg – not only rocks, it melts. Kittiwakes croon lullabies. Mother has a habit of skittishly disappearing into the water. And while predators are few, the ones that do sneak by for a visit – such as orcas – have appallingly big teeth.

Anthropomorphism aside, the harbor seal's life is a stunning example of adaptation to a very particular, limited, and unstable environment. It's also a reminder that ecosystems contain not only living elements, but non-living ones as well. For the seal, glacier ice is a key – if only partially understood – component of survival.

Harbor seals were hunted commercially along Alaska's coasts for nearly a century. One 1955 hunt by two bounty hunters in Aialik Bay yielded 800 seals – more than today's entire population in that bay. The commercial seal hunt ended in 1972, but populations are imperiled more than ever.

Since 1980, the number of seals near Aialik Glacier has decreased approximately 85 percent, from more than 1,600 to about 230 seals. This steep decline coincides with a widespread decline of seals and sea lions throughout the western Gulf of Alaska. Natural cycles might be part of the big picture. In the last few years, the cycle seems to be swinging into another phase. The number of harbor seals at Tugidak Island, near Kodiak, has risen. Yet at Aialik, the population shows no sign of recovery. What's different about these seals, in this very special place?

Members of the "true seal" or Phocidae family, harbor seals feed at sea and rest on land, usually favoring the same environments as humans, including beaches, estuaries, and even manmade piers. In some areas of the Kenai Fjords, however, harbor seals are more selective. In Aialik Bay and Northwestern Fjord, they pup, molt, and rest on ice.

For two weeks in late May and early June, single pups are born on icebergs, usually 5 to 15 feet across. Each pup is born precocious, able to see and swim within an hour. While berg life provides some protection from predators and some flipper room, allowing mother-pup pairs to spread out, it's not exactly nuisance free. Researcher Anne Hoover-Miller once counted up to three eagles and 57 gulls on a pupping berg, scavenging the birthing remains and even pecking at the pup itself.

After a first swim of several minutes, during which a pup may hitch rides on its mother's back, the mother locates another iceberg on which she and her pup can haul out. Mother-pup bonding during the first sensitive hours is followed by three to six weeks of nursing. When ice is largely absent or scattered by winds – as it was over several days in June 1979 – pups face even more challenges. Given the choice between hauling out on rock and swimming, most favored the water. Many mother-pup pairs were separated, and only half as many pups survived to weaning age.

Ice cover varies from year to year, an environmental stress of particular interest in this era of glacial retreat. Hoover-Miller is interested in yet another stress – the impact of human visitation. Using remotely controlled video cameras mounted at the head of Aialik Bay, she can observe iceberg distribution and seal behavior, keeping a keen eye trained to how seals respond when motorized boats and kayaks approach. The answers aren't yet in, but finding a way to study wild animals without disturbing them is just one hopeful step toward solving many Gulf of Alaska puzzles.

Common murres are the concierges of the alcid family, silent except for the occasional nasal moan, and frequently seen lined up, in stoic single file, on cliff ledges. Their heads and backs are tuxedo-tail black; their out-thrust chests and bellies fresh-pressed white. Murres took a beating from the 1989 *Exxon Valdez* oil spill, but their populations on the Chiswell Islands seem to be stable now, at around 3,000 adult breeding birds.

While puffins and common murres congregate in large numbers, some other alcids are more commonly seen in pairs or small groups. The parakeet auklet, half a puffin's size, enjoys its own gustatory niche among the alcids; it eats jellyfish. The rest of the alcid family includes pigeon guillemots, marbled murrelets, Kittlitz's murrelets, ancient murrelets, thick-billed murres, and rhinoceros auklets.

A non-birder might disregard them as "just some gulls," but black-legged kittiwakes make their presence known, wheeling and shrieking. In numbers – perhaps 13,000 along the Kenai Fjords coast – they rival only the tufted puffins. The mostly pale gray and white kittiwakes can be scared into flight by peregrine falcons. These solitary cliff-dwellers hunt high in the air, swooping down upon their smaller bird prey. Bald eagles also nest throughout the Kenai Fjords. Other seabirds include the double-crested, pelagic, and red-face cormorants; black oystercatchers; mew and glaucous-winged gulls; and arctic terns.

Joining the Feast

The sea's bounty is mostly invisible to us, but a whale sighting is one sign that life is as rich below the surface as bird colonies are rowdy above it. During long Alaska summer days, the sun's energy spurs plankton growth in cool, oxygen-rich waters.

A common stop for wildlife tours is the Chiswell Islands at the mouth of Aialik Bay. These six islands are home to thousands of seabirds and a Steller sea lion haul-out and pupping area. The islands are part of the extensive Alaska Maritime National Wildlife Refuge system, which includes some 2,500 islands, headlands, and offshore rocks.

Dall's porpoises sometimes ride the bow waves of tour boats. Clockwise from bottom: Horned puffins, bald eagle, and common murres.

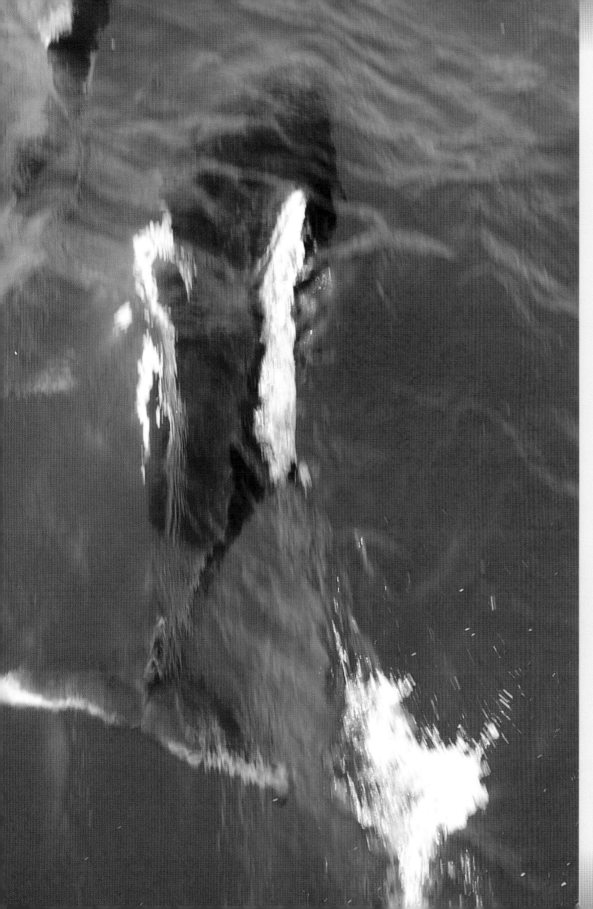

Sea otter (*Enhydra lutris*)

Steller sea lion (*Eumetopias jubatus*)

Harbor seal (*Phoca vitulina*)

Killer whale (*Orcinus orca*)

Harbor porpoise (*Phocoena phocoena*)

Dall's porpoise (*Phocoenides dalli*)

Gray whale (*Eschrichtius robustus*)

Fin whale (*Balaenoptera physalus*)

Minke whale (*Balaenoptera acutorostrata*)

Humpback whale (*Megaptera novaeangliae*)

Sei whale (*Balaenoptera borealis*)

Double-crested cormorant (*Phalacrocorax auritus*)

Bald eagle (*Haliaeetus leucocephalus*)

Black oystercatcher (*Haematopus bachmani*)

Mew gull (*Larus canus*)

Glaucous-winged gull (*Larus glaucescens*)

Black-legged kittiwake (*Rissa tridactyla*)

Arctic tern (*Sterna paradisaea*)

Common murre (*Uria aalge*)

Thick-billed murre (*Uria lomvia*)

Pigeon guillemot (*Cepphus columba*)

Marbled murrelet (*Brachyramphus marmoratus*)

Kittlitz's murrelet (*Brachyramphus brevirostris*)

Parakeet auklet (*Cyclorrhynchus psittacula*)

Rhinoceros auklet (*Cerorhinca monocerata*)

Horned puffin (*Fratercula croniculata*)

Tufted puffin (*Fratercula cirrhata*)

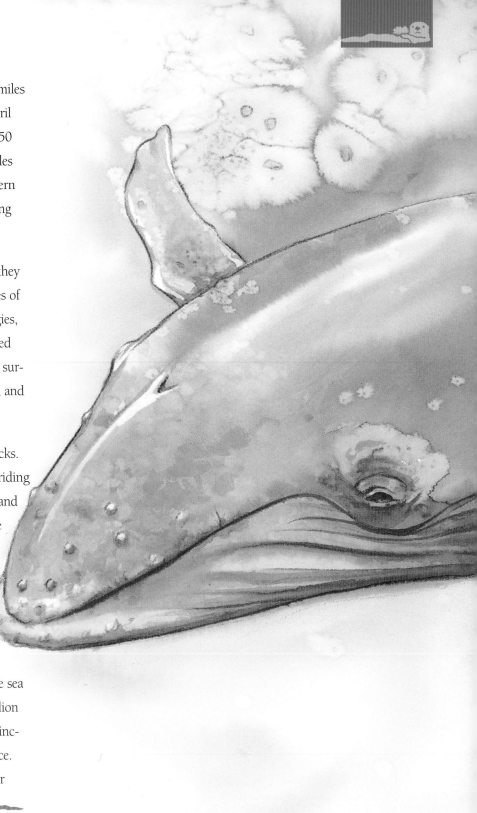

Migratory gray and humpback whales both travel thousands of miles to sample this rich "buffet." Gray whales arrive in March and April from their nursery grounds in Baja California, Mexico. At up to 50 feet long, they are about the same size as humpbacks. Gray whales consume a thousand pounds of food per day during their northern migrations. Unlike other baleen whales, grays eat bottom-dwelling crustaceans.

Humpbacks migrate from Hawaii and Mexico to Alaska, where they linger both alongside and inside the fjords, sieving vast quantities of plankton and small fish. One of their cooperative feeding strategies, called bubble-netting, involves circling fish with a "net" of exhaled bubbles, making the confused prey easier to swallow. Above the surface, humpbacks' acrobatic feats include spyhopping, breaching, and slapping the water with their flukes.

At 30 feet long, minke whales are about half as long as humpbacks. Smaller yet, Dall's porpoises travel in playful pods, occasionally riding the bow wakes of tour boats. Shy harbor porpoises avoid boats and feed closer to shore. Deep within the fjords, harbor seals ride ice floes, while at the fjords' mouths, Steller sea lions bask on algae-slick island ledges. Keeping a keen eye on all of them, orcas travel in pods, surfacing with misty exhalations.

Sea otters prefer to forage for shellfish in waters less than 100 feet deep, which limits them to coves and island margins. While most marine mammals rely on blubber to keep warm, the sea otter uses its dense coat, estimated to have more than a half-million hairs for every square inch. Sea otters were hunted nearly to extinction by Russians and the American profiteers that took their place. Since 1911, when commercial hunting was banned, the sea otter has struggled to make a comeback along the outer coast.

Until the early 1900s, Alutiiq peoples hunted whales. Unlike Bering Sea peoples, who harpooned and towed whales to shore using large open boats, Alutiiq whalers used slender poison-tipped darts or spears to paralyze their prey, and then waited for the dead whale to wash ashore. One poison was derived from monkshood, mixed with human fat rendered from the corpses of prominent people or other whalers. This human fat gave the poison its magical potency.

41

Orca Mysteries

Until the 1970s, people feared the orca, or killer whale, mistakenly assuming that it would attack humans. Long before that, Alutiiq people respected the orca, but even they associated it with death. When an orca came near a village, it was believed to be a deceased person returning in the whale's body, calling another villager to the afterworld. The Latin genus name, "*orcinus,*" means "of or belonging to the realms of the dead."

Time has softened the reputation of orcas, but new discoveries have only increased the aura of mystery surrounding these versatile hunters. Because they hunt in packs, orcas have been called the wolves of the sea. In a different way, documented only in the last three decades, the whales can be compared to bears.

Just as there are two types of bears in the Kenai Fjords, there are two types of orcas, which do not appear to socialize or interbreed. The first group, residents, eat fish. Residents live in extended matrilineal families called pods. They are noisy and gregarious, singing in pod-specific dialects as they cruise open channels and bays. While their name might imply it, these orcas are not strictly homebodies. Resident pods travel hundreds of miles between Prince William Sound, the Kenai Fjords, and Kodiak Island.

The second group, transients, present a more enigmatic picture. Transients are marine mammal hunters. Seals and sea lions are their favored foods, though – to scientists' regret – these orcas are only rarely witnessed consuming their prey. The transients are quieter and stealthier, preferring coves and narrow inlets. Researchers sometimes lose orcas when the whales steer into ice-choked waters where larger boats can't follow. In Aialik Bay, Park Ranger Jim Pfeiffenberger once watched a group of three orcas systematically jostle an iceberg in order to devour a harbor seal.

In the entire Gulf of Alaska, scientists have tallied over 300 resident orcas and 30 transients. (A third, rarely observed group, called "off-shores," is believed to eat high-seas fish and squid.) Few as they are, the transients are suspects in the region's greatest mystery: "Where have all the Steller sea lions gone?"

The western population of Steller sea lions, listed as endangered since 1997, has crashed by more than 80 percent over four decades, from about 180,000 in the 1960s to about 34,000. Hundreds of scientists are searching for culprits in the sea lion decline, with natural environmental change and overfishing heading the list. Another controversial theory suggests that transient orcas eat enough marine mammals – including not only the Stellers, but seals and sea otters, too – to significantly alter those populations. Far from proven, the theory only shows how little we know about this elusive and charismatic whale.

Orca researcher Craig Matkin has logged 20 years photographing dorsal fins, lowering hydrophones into the water, taking genetic samples and assembling orca family trees. Matkin and colleagues have found that at least four pods use the fjords regularly. One of these, AK Pod, has a particular affection for beach rubbing, a rare and fascinating whale behavior. Orcas swim into shallow water a few yards from shore and rub their bodies against the bottom. Not any beach will do, though. The whales require steep slopes, pebbles with diameters of a few inches or less, and no human disturbance.

A New Century in Seward

Frank with Captain Manning, Chirikof Island, 1913. This is one of the few photos of Franklin G. Lowell, probably taken during a visit with his daughter Eva and grandson Frank Revell, Jr. on Chirikof Island, shortly after Katmai volcano erupted in 1912.

The 1880s were a time of quiet endings and new beginnings. The company store at Yalik closed shop. Following relocation of residents to villages farther west, the outer coast's last known permanent village fell off the map.

East of the fjords, a new town, Seward, began to take shape. In 1883, Frank Lowell, a homesteader from Maine, settled near the head of the Resurrection Bay with his wife Mary, a woman of mixed Native-Russian ancestry, from Nanwalek. After a decade of leading fur-hunting expeditions into the fjords, Frank left, but Mary and her children stayed.

In 1902, Mary Lowell sold the rights to her family's homestead to a developer, John Ballaine. Ballaine's dream was to connect the coast with the state's interior via railroad along a route that would be "an all-American route through all-American territory to develop all of Alaska." In 1903, the town of Seward was founded.

As ships discharged railroad workers and roads spread north, homesteaders trickled into town. Their attempts to tame the land didn't take them far from Seward, though. The coastline to the south and west was too barren and steep for farming. Yet what the coast did provide – splendid isolation; fish and fur; the slim chance of mineral discovery – attracted a different sort of entrepreneur.

During Prohibition, which started earlier and lasted later in Alaska than in the nation at large, moonshiners operated from several locations in or near today's Park. On the other side of the law, bounty hunting provided some hardy types with a reason to travel the fjords; the state of Alaska paid its residents $2 to shoot eagles and harbor seals, considered nuisance animals because they competed with humans for fish.

Mary Lowell's granddaughter, also named Mary (William's daughter) standing with Christian Anderson, a child who may have accompanied the earlier surveyors who arrived in 1902 to lay out the town of Seward.

Mary Lowell

While the fog shrouding some aspects of Kenai Fjords history has lifted, we still know little about some of its hardiest pioneers. Mary Lowell's story helps us imagine the challenges faced by a woman living on the Kenai Peninsula coast over a century ago. Even more significantly, it reminds us of the countless other Native women whose stories have remained unrecorded.

Sometime before 1871, when their oldest daughter Anna was born, fur trading agent Frank Lowell met Mary Forgal from English Bay (now Nanwalek). Mary would have been about 16 when she married Frank. Little is known of her earlier years. There are no records of Mary's and Frank's marriage, which produced eight or nine children. In 1883 or 1884, the couple, their children, and several Natives from English Bay (perhaps Mary's relatives) settled at the head of Resurrection Bay.

It is understandable that Frank Lowell needed a Native wife and partner. Union with a Native woman gained Frank a firm alliance with local Native families and cemented his trading ties. Native women's skills made them valuable wives: they knew how to trap small game, gather edibles, and prepare skins and footwear. Frank Lowell's story illustrates the continued dependence of fur traders on the Native community – a story that began with Russian occupation in the eighteenth century.

The Lowell family's decision to move from English Bay, the center of the fur trade, probably was influenced by several local events. In 1883, an influenza epidemic swept through the Kenai Peninsula, taking hundreds of lives. The same year, Mt. Augustine, a volcano across Cook Inlet, erupted and covered villages in ash. A tidal wave flooded English Bay. Thus, in addition to the incentive to start a new fur-trading post, the Lowells may have wished to leave English Bay behind.

Within just a few years, however, the fur trade industry was on the verge of collapse. Sea otter catches were declining; the few animals found in the outer fjords were disappearing from years of overhunting. Frank Lowell was forced to take a post as general agent of the Wrangell Station on the Alaska Peninsula, while Mary and their children stayed in Resurrection Bay. Frank married another Native woman, Akilina Koshon, in 1895. Even after Wrangell Station closed, Frank did not return to Seward.

Mary Lowell died in 1906, from pleurisy. Many geographical features bear her and her family members' names, including Lowell Point, Lowell Canyon, and Mount Eva and Mount Alice (named for two of her daughters); all are within sight of the original Lowell Homestead on the shore of Resurrection Bay.

One of the longest-lived outer coast occupations was fox farming. Edward and Josephine Tuerck (later Sather) founded one of the best-known operations on Nuka Island in 1921. There, they fed the unpenned blue foxes on salmon, seal and sea lion, and even whale meat. After Edward Tuerck died, Josephine married "Herring Pete" Sather. Pete helped keep the farm running, but he was famous along the outer coast for all the other jobs he juggled: fishing and mining, as well as transporting other miners, hunters, sightseers, mail and freight between Seward and Nuka Bay. Where Russian mother ships had once plied the coast, Herring Pete's gasboat chugged for years, stitching together the lives of many coastal residents. Fox fur prices rose and fell many times over the decades, and the Sather operation lasted longer than most. By the 1950s, pelts were practically worthless, but out of affection for their animals, the couple continued to feed some foxes for several more years.

Pete Sather's life was a microcosm of outer coast life in the last century. Like the Unegkurmiut who came before him, he survived by being a generalist – a wandering jack-of-all-trades, appreciative of nature but just as eager to trap, fish and mine. He was at home on the sea; in 1964 a reporter described him as "a man who can't stand dry land." But the bountiful ocean takes as much as it gives away. On a stormy trip between Nuka Island and Seward in 1961, Herring Pete disappeared.

Creating the Park

Some of the coast's earliest American visitors were its most prescient. Geologists U.S. Grant and D.F. Higgins, who mapped the glaciers and coast in 1909, enthused in print a few years later: "It is hoped that this publication may attract attention to some of the most magnificent scenery that is now accessible to the tourist and nature lover."

Traces of human activity, like this closed mine at Nuka Bay (left), still mark the Kenai Fjords, but lush coastal growth has obscured many reminders of the region's human past. Devil's club (below), is one spiny coastal shrub that humbles the modern hiker. While the plant's berries are considered toxic, Native Alaskans use extracts and poultices of the plant to treat many illnesses.

Sampling of Species

Common cowparsnip (*Heracleum lanatum*)

Devils club (*Oplopanax horridus*)

Bunchberry dogwood (*Cornus Canadensis*)

Field horsetail (*Equisetum arvense*)

Wintergreen (*Pyrola chlorantha*)

Marsh lupine (*Lupinus polyphyllus*)

Mountain alder (*Alnus viridis ssp. crispa*)

Fireweed (*Epilobium augustifolium*)

Dwarf fireweed (*Epilobium latifolium*)

White spruce (*Picea glauca*)

Black spruce (*Picea mariana*)

Sitka spruce (*Picea sitchensis*)

Alpine hemlock (*Tsuga mertensiana*)

Common ladyfern (*Athyrium filix-femina*)

Dark-throat shooting star (*Dodecatheon pulchellum*)

Larkspur leaf monkshood (*Aconitum delphiniifolum*)

Red baneberry (*Actaea rubra*)

Crimson columbine (*Aquilegia Formosa*)

Mountain larkspur (*Delphininum glaucum*)

Prickly rose (*Rosa acicularis*)

Balsam poplar (*Populus balsamifera ssp. trichocarpa*)

Quaking aspen (*Populus tremuloides*)

Feltleaf willow (*Salix alaxensis var. longistylis*)

Northern groundcone (*Boschniakia rossica*)

Common monkeyflower (*Mimulus guttatus*)

Jacob's ladder (*Polemonium pulcherriumum*)

Adapted to withstand severe weather and thin soil, ground-hugging wildflowers bloom profusely from May through August. Clockwise from top: Wild iris, anemone, Nootka lupine.

Hunters aside, tourists were slow to discover Resurrection Bay, and even slower to brave boating and hiking trips into today's Park. Sportfishermen trickled into the fjords over many decades. It took a band of eager local citizens – including Herman Leirer and Jack Werner – to rally efforts to build a road inland to Exit Glacier. The project, started in 1965, wasn't fully completed until 1986, when a final vehicle bridge over Resurrection River was opened to traffic. Harding Icefield wasn't crossed by mountaineers until 1968. But that conquest opened the floodgates, with sightseeing plane charters and icefield ski-doo rentals to follow. One controversial development scenario – thwarted by nature and permitting problems – involved the construction of a $1.5 million icefield attraction, including gondola lift system and summit station.

Through the efforts of local entrepreneurs and the sheer magnetism of the coast itself, the future Park's eclectic attractions, resources and unparalleled beauty were becoming better known. At the same time, land managers were eager to take advantage of the Alaska Native Claims Settlement Act (ANCSA) passed in 1971, which both resolved Native land claims and allowed for the creation of new national park, national forest, and national wildlife refuge units. In 1978, President Carter created the Kenai Fjords National Monument. Two years later, the area was designated a national park.

Its geological and human history make Kenai Fjords National Park one of the most ancient and pristine places that some visitors will ever see. But compared to many parks, Kenai Fjords National Park is still new. Dolly Varden were recently discovered in Exit Creek, once thought to be too silty for fish to colonize. Retreating glaciers uncover old forests while they make way for new ones to grow. Protected for future generations, the Park continues to reveal itself – one vista, one species, one scoured foot of bedrock at a time.

Rockwell
Kent

A different kind of visitor, seeking peace and refuge instead of profit, visited Resurrection Bay in 1918. Renowned artist-illustrator Rockwell Kent and his 9-year-old son spent three seasons enjoying a "quiet adventure" on remote Fox Island. The island stay would prove to be a turning point in Kent's life. Father and son were aided during their self-imposed isolation by an aging trapper named Olson. But nature, in the form of birds and foxes, waves and brutally cold winds, was their closest companion. Kent's inspired memoir, *Wilderness: A Journal of Quiet Adventure in Alaska* is illustrated with the woodcut engravings he made on Fox Island.

"I crave snow-topped mountains, dreary wastes, and the cruel Northern sea with its far horizons at the edge of the world where infinite space begins. Here skies are clearer and deeper and, for the greater wonders they reveal, a thousand times more eloquent of the eternal mystery than those of softer lands."

—Rockwell Kent